Let's Take A Walk Through Our Orthodox Church

by
Anthony M. Coniaris

Illustrated by Betty Kizilos

LIGHT & LIFE PUBLISHING
Minneapolis, Minnesota

Light and Life Publishing
P.O. Box 26421
Minneapolis, MN 55426-0421

Copyright © 1998
Anthony M. Coniaris
Library of Congress No. 98-92087

ISBN 1-880971-39-9

Table of Contents

Introduction

When we come to worship in the Orthodox Church, we are surrounded by a variety of objects that conspire to keep our attention focused on the worship of God.

Icons, architecture, candles, incense, votive lights, chandeliers, and vestments all speak to us in their own way to tell us something about our faith.

This book takes a child on a tour through an Orthodox Church, clearly and simply explaining in forty-five brief chapters the meaning of many objects seen in most Orthodox Churches.

Each explanation is enhanced with an original four-color painting.

The book is written primarily for children in grades 3 through 6. It is excellent for use by parents at home, by church school teachers, and by priests.

The Church Building

The **church building** is God's house.

Because God is the King of Kings, the house of God is built to look like a palace.

A palace is a very beautiful building where the king lives. Oftentimes there is a gold dome on top of the church. Gold is a color used for kings.

We go to church because God is more than a king for us. He is our loving Father. We go to church because we belong there.

We are members of God's kingly or royal family. Each of us is a prince or princess in God's eyes.

Because we belong to God, we are very important people. The more we love God, the more we want to go to His palace to be with Him.

We go to church to pray, to listen to God's word, to receive His Presence in Holy Communion.

When we go to church something wonderful happens. Each of us becomes a palace or temple of God's presence.

This happens because God comes to live in us.

The name of my church is _____ Church.

The name of my priest is Father _____ .

I was glad when they said to me, let us go into the house of the Lord. (Psalm 12:1)

Each of us becomes a temple
when God comes to live in us.

Two Angels at the Door

In some Orthodox Churches the icons of **two angels** are painted on the walls by the doors to the church. They are holding two scrolls or long pads of paper.

Their work is to write down the names of those who come to church to worship God.

God knows when we come to church. His holy angels keep a record for Him.

He is very pleased when He sees us there.

We go to church on Sunday because that is where we belong as God's children. The church is our home.

When God opens the book of life on the last day, how many times will He see your name there?

Surely goodness and love will follow me all the days of my life, and I will dwell in the house of the Lord forever (Psalm 23:6).

God's holy angels keep a record.

The Narthex

The first place we come to when we go into the church is called the **narthex**.

The narthex is like a porch or entry way that one comes to before going into a house.

When we are in the narthex we are still in this world.

When we walk from the narthex into the nave, or church, we are going from this world into God's house or His kingdom.

In the narthex there is an icon of Jesus to whose house we have come.

He stands at the door as the host to greet us because He is happy when we come to His house.

To show our love for Him, we make the sign of the cross and kiss His icon.

As we kiss Jesus' icon we must remember that He is also kissing us back. He loves us even more than we love him.

After kissing the icon we light a candle.

This helps us remember that Jesus wants us to shine as lights for Him in this dark world.

Let your light so shine before people, that they may see your good works and give glory to your father who is in heaven (Matt. 5:16).

Jesus stands at the door of the church to greet us.

Making the Sign of the Cross

Orthodox Christians make the **sign of the cross**. We join the two index fingers and the thumb of the right hand to show that we believe in:

      – God the Father who loves us,

      – God the Son (Jesus) who saves us,

      – God the Holy Spirit who lives in us.

The three fingers are joined together to show that we believe in one God, not three. The other two fingers remind us that Jesus was both God and man at the same time. We drop the two fingers into the palm of the hand to show that Jesus "came down from heaven" to save us.

Making the sign of the cross reminds us of the great price Jesus paid to save us from sin. It tells us of His great love for us.

When making the sign of the cross, we pray: "In the name of the Father (as we touch our forehead) and of the Son (as we touch our chest) and of the Holy Spirit (as we touch first our right and then our left shoulder).

When we make the sign of the cross, we are also telling God that we love Him "with all our mind" as we touch our forehead; "with all our strength" as we touch our shoulders; and "with all our heart" as we touch our chest.

When we make the sign of the cross, we are praying not only with our mind and heart, but also with our body.

> *... and you shall love the Lord your God with all your heart, and with all your soul, and with all your might (Deut. 6:4).*

**Orthodox Christians pray with their bodies
as they cross themselves.**

The Icon of the Mother of God on the Front Wall

As we look at the front wall behind the holy table, we see a very large **icon or holy picture of the Mother of God** holding the Christ Child in her arms.

This icon has an important message for us. It tells us that our purpose in life as Christians is to have Christ come and live in us as He came to live in His Mother.

It is as if the Mother of God on the front wall is saying to us, "Look, the Great God has become small. He comes to you as a baby. He wants you to take Him into your arms and into your heart. I am holding Him in my arms because I wish to give Him to you. Come, take Him from my arms as St. Symeon did in the temple. Put your arms around Him. Cradle Him. Love Him. Hug Him. Obey Him. Follow Him. In Him you will find love, forgiveness, joy and eternal life."

Jesus was born in His Mother when she heard the word of God and obeyed it.

The same Jesus comes to live in us, too, when we hear and obey His word as His Mother did.

The Mother of God is not on the front wall so that we may pray **to** her, but **with** her to her Son. She is like the leader of a choir leading all of us in prayer to her Son.

Let each of us take Jesus from the arms of His Mother and carry Him into our hearts and lives.

> *It is not I who lives, but Christ who lives in me. (Galatians 2:20)*

Each of us should take Jesus from the arms of His Mother and carry Him in our hearts and lives.

Icons

When we go into an Orthodox Church, we see **icons** or holy pictures everywhere.

An icon is like a window that helps us look into heaven. It shows us the holy people, or saints, who lived before us. They are now in heaven where they pray for us. Icons also show us the miracles of Jesus and all that He did for us.

If someone who does not believe in God, asks you what you believe, take him into church and show him the icons. This is like "show-and-tell" at school. Icons show and tell what we believe.

We do not worship icons. We worship God. Icons help us to worship and honor God.

When we stand in church and see all the icons of Christ and the saints, we feel that we are not alone. We feel that we are part of **God's family**. All the saints are our brothers and sisters. We, too, are called to be saints—God's holy people.

Because each one of us is made in the image of God, we, too, are icons. The word **image** means icon (picture). We are living icons of Christ. Other people are also living icons of God. That is why we treat them with even more love and respect than we do the wooden icons.

An icon is not fully an icon until it is blessed by the priest in church. Then it becomes a place of prayer where we meet Christ and pray to Him.

If icons are windows to heaven, let us use them often to peek into heaven.

> *God made man in his own image, in the image of God, he created him (Genesis 1:27).*

Icons are windows to heaven.

The Pantocrator Christ in the Dome

A large icon of Christ is placed in the middle of the dome. It is called the **Pantocrator**, or the **Almighty One**.

With His left hand, Jesus, the Almighty One, holds the Gospel book which has in it the words He spoke and the great works He did for us.

He wants us to read this book, the Holy Bible, so that He may speak to us His words of Life.

With His right hand Jesus blesses those who have come to His holy house.

Jesus looks down on us from the dome to let us know that His eye is always upon us.

He is always there to hear our prayers, to lead us, to guide us, to help us.

Even when we are at home in our bedroom or at school or at play, we should remember that the same Jesus who looks upon us in church from the dome is still hovering above us, just a prayer away from us.

We can never escape from His presence.

When we receive His Body and Blood in Holy Communion, He comes down from the dome and lives in our hearts.

Jesus hovers above us not only in church but wherever we are.

Lo, I am with you always, to the close of the age (Matt. 28:20).

Jesus hovers above us wherever we are.

How the Icons are Placed in Church

The **icons are placed on the walls of the church in a very special way**. The highest place in the dome is kept for our Lord.

Just below the icon of Christ in the dome are placed the prophets who told us beforehand that Christ—the Messiah and Savior—would come to us.

Below the prophets are placed the twelve disciples of Jesus, with a special place for the four gospel writers: Matthew, Mark, Luke, and John.

On the front wall of the Church is the icon of the Mother of God holding the Christ Child.

On the upper part of the Iconostasion, the holy altar screen, are usually placed twelve icons of the most important events (happenings) in the life of Jesus (the Twelve Great Feasts). Not all churches may have this exact arrangement.

The ground floor of the church stands for this world. We who are still in this world stand on the ground floor, but we can look up at the dome and the walls to see what great things God has done for us. When we do this, it helps us to remember God's great love for us. We see what He has done to save us from sin and death and to make us His children.

When we look up in church we see heaven.

Therefore, since we are surrounded by so great a cloud of witnesses ... let us look to Jesus who has taken His seat at the right hand of the throne of God (Heb. 12.1-2).

When we look up in church we see heaven.

The Altar Table

The **altar table** stands just behind the royal door. It is raised from the floor of the church by a few steps. This shows that the purpose of the altar is to raise us up to heaven.

The early Christians did not have churches because they were persecuted for believing in Christ.

They worshiped God secretly in underground caves (catacombs). This is where they also buried their dead.

When they celebrated the liturgy, they would use as an altar table the tomb of someone who had given his or her life for Christ. Such a person is called a **martyr**.

When the bishop comes to bless (consecrate) a new church, he places tiny pieces of the remains (bones) of a martyr or saint inside the altar. He does this to remind us that the church was built on the blood of the martyrs.

The martyrs gave their all for the church. God expects us to be like the martyrs—ready to help His work through the church by giving the best of our time, talents, and possessions (what we have).

Jesus gathered around a table with His apostles for the Last Supper. So, He gathers with us today around the altar table to feed us His precious Body and Blood (Holy Communion). This happens every time we come to the liturgy.

The altar is a place of sacrifice. It reminds us to give our best for God's work through our gifts to the church.

Let us commit ourselves, and one another, and our whole life to Christ our God – Orthodox Liturgy

So He gathers with us at the holy table today.

The Cross

Behind the holy altar is a large **cross** with the body of Christ on it.

The cross shows how much God loves us. Jesus stretches His arms out on the cross as if to tell us, "This is how much I love you!".

The body is removed from the cross once every year on Holy Friday. It is wrapped in a sheet and placed in a tomb that is decorated with flowers. It is placed back on the cross forty days after Easter on the Day of Ascension. This is the day that Jesus ascended (went up) into heaven.

Tradition tells us that the cross on which Jesus was crucified was anchored on top of Adam's tomb. Thus, Adam was the first to be baptized in the blood and water that flowed from the side of Jesus on the cross (John 19:34).

Many icons of the crucified Christ show water and blood flowing from the body of Jesus onto the skull of Adam which is seen at the foot of the cross.

Thus, the first to sin, Adam, was the first to be cleansed by the blood of Jesus.

We, too, are cleansed by the blood of Jesus when we receive Holy Communion.

The water from the side of Jesus flows upon us in holy baptism when it cleanses us of sin and makes us children of God.

"Each one of us is the person for whom Jesus shed that particular drop of blood," said Blaise Pascal.

> *For God so loved the world that He gave His only Son, so that whoever believes in Him should not perish but have eternal life (John 3:16).*

**Adam was the first to be baptized in the blood and
water that flowed from Jesus' side.**

The Votive Light

One sees many vigil or **votive lights** in an Orthodox Church.

A votive or vigil light is made up of three things: the wax or oil, the wick, and the flame.

The wax or oil that feeds the wick and keeps it burning is really our prayers. This includes the Sacraments, the Bible, and the liturgy.

The wick is the spirit of man or the soul. The Bible says, "The spirit of man is the candle of the Lord" (Proverbs 20:27). The flame or fire is the Holy Spirit Who lights the wick of our spirit and keeps it aflame for Christ.

Vigil lights will be seen hanging in front of icons of the saints. This is to show that, without the light Who is Christ, the saints are nothing. It is only as the light of Christ shines in them that the saints come alive and shine as living icons of Christ.

The Bible says that God is fire. Through the Holy Spirit He looks for material to set on fire with His love. We are that material. Jesus came to light the lamp of love in each person's soul.

Let us always protect this inner lamp.

Let us keep the wick burning through prayer.

Let the Holy Spirit light the fire of His presence in the fireplace of your soul.

Become a living candle for the Lord. Shine for Him. Light the fire of God's presence in yourself and in others. Then people will feel the warmth of God's presence in us.

> *The spirit of man is the candle of the Lord (Prov. 20:27).*

26

Shine as a living candle for the Lord.

The Iconostasion or Icon Screen

The first level of the **icon screen** has six icons, three on either side of the royal door. The large, middle opening is called the **Royal Door** because the Body and Blood of Christ, Who is King, is carried through that door when the priest brings Holy Communion to the people.

The first icon on the right side of the Royal Door is always that of our Lord Jesus Christ. The icon on the right of Jesus is always that of St. John the Baptist. He is the last of the Old Testament prophets. The prophets foretold the coming of Christ hundreds of years before it happened. St. John is usually pointing his finger to Jesus on his right as if to tell us that Jesus is truly the expected Messiah or the Christ. It is as if through the person of St. John the entire Old Testament is pointing to Jesus and saying, "Jesus is the expected Messiah. Behold the Lamb of God, who takes away the sins of the world."

The first icon on the left of the Royal Door is always that of the Mother of God holding the Christ Child.

The icon to the left of the Theotokos is different from church to church. This is the icon of the saint or sacred event after which the church is named. If the church were named after St. Nicholas, there would be an icon of St. Nicholas in this panel.

The two end panels of the icon screen are doors that open into the altar. On these doors are painted icons of the Archangels Michael and Gabriel. They stand guard at the entrance to the holy of holies, which is the altar or sanctuary. Only persons who are specially blessed by the bishop such as priests, deacons, acolytes, and readers are allowed to enter the altar area.

The Royal Door reminds us that Jesus is the door that leads to the Father.

> *Jesus said, "No one comes to the Father but by Me"* *(John 14:6).*

28

The icon screen and altar

The Tabernacle

The tabernacle is a beautifully decorated container that stands in the middle of the altar table. In the Old Testament the tablets on which God had written the Ten Commandments were kept in the tabernacle. The tabernacle itself was kept in the Holy of Holies of the Temple in Jerusalem. It was very sacred. It reminded people of the presence of God. People were not allowed to go near it. The word tabernacle means a place where God lives.

In our church it is the Lord Jesus Himself who is present in the tabernacle. His Body and Blood are always kept in the tabernacle on the holy altar table. That is why the church is truly the house of God. God is always present here in a very special way. This is why we always bow and make the sign of the cross whenever we pass before the tabernacle.

In addition to the Body and Blood of Christ, the holy oil of Chrismation is kept in the tabernacle. This is the oil with which the newly baptized are anointed in order to receive the gift of the Holy Spirit. The oil of holy unction which is used for healing the sick is also kept in the tabernacle as well as holy water that is blessed on the Feast of Epiphany. Holy Communion is kept in the tabernacle for the sick who cannot come to church. The priest takes it to them. The tabernacle is indeed the most sacred object in the church. Unlike the people who lived before Christ, however, we are allowed to come close to the tabernacle. In fact, the same Jesus who lives in the tabernacle moves out of the tabernacle and comes to make His home in our hearts when we receive His precious Body and Blood in Holy Communion. We become His living tabernacles. When we were anointed with the holy oil of Chrismation at baptism, we became living temples of the Holy Spirit. We are also anointed with holy unction for healing when we are sick, and are blessed with holy water each year on the Feast of Epiphany. We are just as holy as the tabernacle because the same God who is in the tabernacle comes to live in us.

> *Do you not know that your body is a temple of the Holy Spirit within you, which you have from God? (1 Cor. 6:19)*

Through faith and the sacraments God comes to live in the tabernacle of our soul.

The Gospel Book

The **Gospel book** is called in Greek, *Evangelion*, which means Good News. It is **God's Good News** book. Bound beautifully in gold or silver, it is kept always on the holy altar table. It is as if the altar table is a throne for the Gospel book. Whenever the priest brings the Gospel book to us we kiss it to show how much we love Jesus and His words.

Christ is always present on the altar table both as the Word of God in the Gospel Book and as the Bread of Life (Holy Communion) in the tabernacle. In each liturgy God gives us two things we need for living. He gives us light to show us the way (the Gospel Book). He gives us also food to keep us alive and growing in Christ (Holy Communion).

It is from this Gospel book that the priest reads God's word to the people in the liturgy. In every liturgy the priest carries the Gospel book out to the people, holds it high, and tells the people that Christ will give us His wisdom when the Gospel is read. He says, "Wisdom! Let us pay attention." He does this in what is called "The Little Entrance."

The front cover of the Gospel book has a picture of the Resurrection of Jesus from the dead. This side always faces up on Saturday and Sunday when we remember the resurrection of Jesus. Every Sunday is a little Easter (Pascha). The back cover of the Gospel book has a picture of the crucifixion of Jesus. This side faces up on the altar table during the rest of the week when we remember His life, suffering, and death.

The four Gospels are part of the Holy Bible. The Bible is God's love letter to us. In this book God tells us how much He loves us. He tells us how He wants us to live. The Bible is like a road map that gives us God's directions for life. When we read the Bible, or a Bible story book, we are letting God speak to us. If we read the Bible, we will always find our way home to God.

Your word is a lamp to my feet and a light to my path (Psalm 119:105).

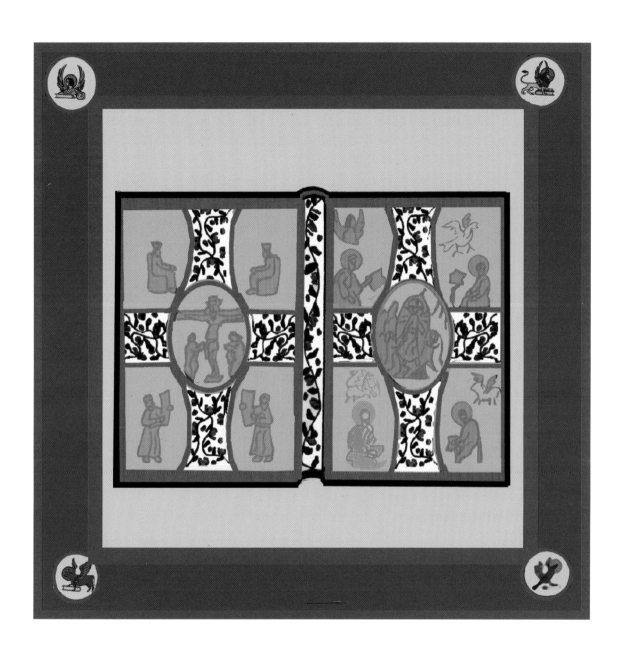

**Through the Gospel Book Jesus continues
to speak to us today.**

The Icon of the Birth Of Jesus

Icons, or holy pictures, tell the story of what we believe.

Let us see how many truths about God just one such icon can give us. Walk around the church until you find **an icon of the birth of Jesus**. This is what you will see:

He who made the whole world becomes one of us as a newborn baby. Though He is a little helpless figure in swaddling clothes, He is still the Lord of Creation. In the icon you will see angels singing praises in the skies above. The Magi and the shepherds bring their gifts. The sky salutes Him with a star. The earth offers Him a cave. The animals look at Him in silent wonder with wide-open eyes. And we humans offer him one of us, the Virgin Mother.

The black color of the cave shows the darkness of the world into which He came to be the light of the world. The scene on the lower right side shows the midwife and her helper washing the baby. This tells us that Jesus was born like any other child.

The scene on the lower left side shows Joseph. He is being tempted by the devil who stands before him.

The devil tells Joseph that if the baby were truly the Son of God, he would not have been born like any other child. The Mother Mary looks at Joseph as if trying to tell him that what the devil is suggesting is not true.

Just one icon tells us all these wonderful truths about the birth of Jesus.

Why did God come to us as a baby? Because, like every baby, He wants to be loved.

I love you, Jesus, with all my mind, heart, soul and strength.

> *For to you is born this day in the City of David a Savior, who is Christ the Lord (Luke 2:11).*

Christ is born. Glorify Him!

The Icon of the Crucifixion

As you continue your walk around the church, look for an **icon of the Crucifixion** of Jesus. You will note that this icon does not frighten us with the cold breath of death. It breathes, instead, the sweet hope of eternal life with God.

Christ is shown as standing on the cross, not hanging on it. The expression on the face of Jesus is not the open mouth of the last spasm of death, full of horror.

It is, rather, a face full of heavenly peace, gentleness, and forgiveness. For this is the suffering Savior who has undone the pangs of death and given us the peace of the life to come.

The crucified body is the very body of the God-Man Himself. It radiates the hope of the Resurrection. The Lord does not hang on the cross like some miserable criminal.

It is He, rather, who appears to be holding up the cross. His hands are not cramped as they are nailed to the wood. Instead, He spreads them out peacefully in an attitude of prayer.

Instead of filling us with the brute horror of death, the entire icon is illuminated by the light of hope in Christ.

It is full of the grace of the Holy Spirit. It breathes the nobility and gentleness of eternal life.

In some icons of the crucifixion, the sun and moon are placed in such a position above the cross as to make it appear that the outstretched hands of the Savior are holding them up.

Jesus is our King. His throne is the cross.

> *He Himself bore our sins in His body on the tree, that we might die to sin and live to righteousness. By His wounds you have been healed (1 Peter 2:24).*

Icon of the Crucifixion

The Icon of the Resurrection

Continue your walk around the church until you come to an **icon of the Resurrection** of Jesus. This is what you will see:

This icon shows what the Resurrection of Jesus really means. It shows the risen Christ descending into the depths of death (Hades).

There He breaks the bonds of death and announces to those who lived in the Old Testament the good news of salvation from sin and death.

We see the broken doors of death flying off their hinges and arranging themselves in the form of a cross.

Then we see the second Adam, Jesus, the perfect Man, bending over an old man.

He takes him by the hand and leads him out of the tomb. That old man is Adam.

With his left hand, Jesus raises Eve out of the tomb, and, behind her, all the righteous patriarchs, prophets, and kings who lived before His coming.

He is indeed the Victorious Christ who has "trampled death by (His) death and to those in the tombs He has given life."

One day the same risen Christ will reach His hand out to you and me. He will raise us from the tomb of death to life everlasting.

Christ is risen from the dead. By His death He has destroyed death and to those in the tombs He has given life (Hymn of Pascha).

Jesus conquered death!

The Eternal Light

The eternal light is a votive light that either hangs from the ceiling above the tabernacle, or burns before it on the altar table.

It is kept burning always to show that the Lord Jesus Christ, Who is "the light of the world," is present in the tabernacle.

Because Jesus died at 3 p.m. on Holy Friday, the eternal light is put out every year at that hour.

It is lit again at the midnight Easter service to remind us that "Christ is Risen, the light shines in the darkness, and the darkness has not overcome it" (John 1:5).

We who live in darkness have now seen the great light—Jesus—who shines as "a lamp to our feet and a light to our path" (Psalm 119:105).

Once you were darkness, but now you are light in the Lord; walk as children of light (Ephesians 5:8).

The Eternal Light tells us that Jesus is the Light of the World

Incense

Orthodox Christians use **incense** when they worship God. The censer itself has a basin in which there is a burning piece of charcoal. A piece of incense is placed on top of the charcoal. This produces a sweet-smelling smoke which stands for our prayers as they rise to God. Psalm 140:2 says, "Let my prayer rise like incense before you...". The sweet-smelling smoke that rises from the censer tells us that our prayers are like perfume to God. He is very pleased when we pray to Him.

The act of burning incense before Jesus is also a way of showing that Jesus is our God. The early Christians would not throw a pinch of incense before the statue of Caesar. That would mean that Caesar was God. For the Christians, Jesus is God. They would offer incense only to Jesus. Because they did not burn incense before Caesar, they were thrown to the lions.

After censing Jesus and the saints, the priest turns to the people and censes each person. By doing this he is paying respect to the image (icon) of God in each one of us.There are twelve bells on the censer. They stand for the twelve apostles who spread the joy of the Gospel to the ends of the earth. The three chains of the censer that hold the basin, stand for the Father Who loves us, the Son Who saves us, and the Holy Spirit Who lives in us.

Many Orthodox families have a home censer which they use when the family prays together. It is kept next to the family icon. As the parents cense the home every Saturday evening, the presence of God fills every room of the house. God is so real in Orthodox worship that He can be **seen** in the icon, **heard** in the Bible reading, **tasted** in Holy Communion, **touched** as we kiss the icon, and **smelled** in the fragrance of the incense. He can be experienced as a living God through all five senses. The fragrance of incense that greets us as we enter church reminds us of Jesus Who "loved us and gave Himself up for us, a fragrant offering and sacrifice to God" (Eph. 5:2).

We are the Aroma (perfume) of Christ to God (St. Paul).

Let my prayer rise as incense before You.

Candles!

Someone once called the Orthodox Church "The Candlelight Kingdom."

We have **candles** at Easter, candles at weddings, candles at baptisms, candles on the altar table, candles before icons, candles everywhere.

Lighting a candle is like praying because we never light a candle without praying.

Lighting a candle reminds us that Jesus is "the light that shines in the darkness and the darkness has not overcome it" (John 1:5).

Lighting a candle reminds us that Jesus is the light of the world. Whoever follows Him does not walk in darkness but has the light of life (John 8:12).

Lighting a candle reminds us to believe in the light and to walk in the light that we may become children of light.

Many Orthodox Christians light a candle when they first come to church. Doing this reminds us that when we were baptized we received Jesus Who is the light of the world.

Like Him we are to be lighting candles of hope and love in the lives of people.

As we light a candle before entering church we can pray the beautiful words of the Psalmist:

> *The Lord is my light and my salvation; whom shall I fear? The Lord is the stronghold of my life; of whom shall I be afraid? (Psalm 27:1).*

Lighting a candle reminds us that we are to be like
lights shining for Jesus.

Candles Go Before the Gospel

When the priest carries the Gospel Book in a procession during the liturgy, the altar servers **carry candles** before him to show that the word of God is a "lamp unto our feet and a light unto our path."

The candles that go before the Gospel Book tell us that the word of God is truly a light for the darkness in which we walk.

The purpose of God's word is to show us the way, to prevent us from stumbling in the darkness, and to lead us home to God.

We need to listen carefully when God's word is being read in church.

We need also to read God's word every day in the holy Bible or a Bible story book. God's word is like a flashlight in the darkness.

St. Isaac the Syrian said, "Reading the word of God is the light of the soul."

The light shines in the darkness and the darkness has not overcome it (John 1:5).

God's word is like a flashlight in the darkness.

The Epitaphion and the Tomb of Jesus

Most Orthodox Churches have a beautiful tomb of Christ sitting in a corner of the sanctuary. Every Good Friday it is decorated with flowers.

On the tomb is placed an **Epitaphion** (in Slavonic, plaschanitsa). This is a rectangular piece of cloth on which is painted the Body of Jesus laid out for burial. The word *Epitaphion* means "something which is placed on top of a tomb." It reminds us of the winding sheet in which Christ's body was wrapped when it was taken down from the cross and laid in the tomb. In addition to the figure of Christ in the tomb, the *Epitaphion* cloth includes pictures of Mary, the Mother of God; Joseph of Arimathea, and the saintly women who took part in the burial of Jesus.

On Good Friday afternoon, the priest, representing Joseph of Arimathea, removes the body of Christ from the cross. He lays it carefully in a shroud or winding sheet. Then he carries it into the altar which stands for the tomb of Jesus.

During the afternoon service of Great and Holy Friday, the priest lifts the *Epitaphion* cloth which has the picture of Jesus lying in the tomb, and carries it in a procession around the church. The Great and Holy Friday evening service takes place around the tomb of Jesus, beautifully decorated with flowers. The *Epitaphion*, showing the Body of Jesus laid out for burial, is placed in the tomb, surrounded with flower petals.

The people gather round the tomb of Jesus and sing a funeral service for Jesus. They express their sorrow over Jesus' death. Yet even in their sorrow they sound the note of the joy of the Resurrection in their singing. Before they leave, the people kiss the Body of Jesus in the tomb. They are all given a flower from the tomb which they take home and keep on their family altar.

We worship Thy passion, O Christ; show us also Your glorious resurrection. – Holy Week Hymn

The Body of Christ is laid out for burial (Epitaphion) on Good Friday

Kollyva: Boiled Wheat at Memorial Services

When Orthodox Christians pray for the dead, they bring a tray of boiled wheat kernels to church for the service. This is called **Kollyva** in Greek.

The wheat kernels show that we believe in life after death.

Jesus said, "Unless a grain of wheat falls into the earth and dies, it remains alone, but if it dies, it brings forth much fruit" (John 12:24).

Just as a new plant rises from the buried kernel of wheat (which is a seed), so we believe that the person buried will rise one day to new life with God.

The wheat kernels are covered with sugar and raisins to show the sweetness of life with God in heaven.

We pray for the dead because we believe they are alive with God.

For as in Adam all die, so in Christ all will be made alive (1 Cor. 15:22).

We pray for the dead because we believe
they are alive with God.

The Pulpit

The **pulpit** is the stand from which the priest reads to us from the Gospels of Matthew, Mark, Luke and John.

The priest also speaks to the people about God from the same pulpit. We call this: "preaching the sermon."

The pulpit reminds us of the big stone that was used to close the tomb of Jesus.

An angel stood on top of this stone on Easter morning. He told the people the good news that Jesus had risen from the dead.

That was very good news! That is why the book from which the priest reads is called the GOOD NEWS BOOK (*Evangelion* in Greek).

When we see the priest going to the pulpit, he is going there to do one of two things: he will either read God's word to us or he will share the good news of God's love for us in a talk or sermon. When this happens, we pay special attention.

We listen carefully because when the priest is at the pulpit, it is as if Jesus is speaking to us.

Man shall not live by bread alone, but by every word that proceeds from the mouth of God (Matt. 4:4).

The angel was the first to speak from above a stone pulpit to announce the good news that CHRIST IS RISEN!

The Chalice

There is a special cup which holds the wine that becomes the blood of Christ. We call it the **chalice**, the cup of salvation. When we kneel during the liturgy, we pray with the priest that God the Holy Spirit may change the bread and wine into the Body and Blood of Jesus. This means that when we come to receive Holy Communion, Jesus comes to live in us.

What should we do to prepare to receive the Body and Blood of Jesus? We should pray. We should have love in our hearts for all people. We should ask forgiveness from God and from our parents, brothers, and sisters. Also from anyone we may have hurt.

When we come before the priest for Communion, we should make the sign of the cross, tell the priest our first name, hold the Communion cloth under our chin, and open our mouth wide. After receiving Communion we should wipe our lips with the Communion cloth, make the sign of the cross, and hand the Communion cloth to the person next to us.

Once we have received Communion, we must remember that we have become one with Christ and with all those who received Communion with us. The same Christ now lives in all of us. We are all living icons of Jesus. It is by loving one another that we love Jesus. After receiving Communion our bodies become holy chalices. God has come to live in us. His blood now flows through our veins.

Jesus wants to use our hands, which have now become His hands, to help those in need. When we receive Communion, we become members of Christ's Body, the Church. This means that Jesus has no eyes but our eyes, no feet but our feet to do His work in the world today. What kind, thoughtful act will you do for Jesus today?

"When we come to receive Communion Jesus kisses us on the lips," said St. Ambrose.

For my flesh is real food and my blood is real drink. Whoever eats my flesh and drinks my blood lives in me and I in him (John 6:55-56).

The Chalice is the Cup of Salvation.

The Blessing of the Five Loaves

You may happen to visit an Orthodox Church at a time when **the blessing of the loaves** is taking place.

You will see a table outside the icon screen with five loaves of bread on it.

These loaves will be blessed by the priest at the end of the service. Then they will be cut into small pieces and given to the people as they leave for home.

The purpose of this service is to remind us of a great miracle that Jesus did one day. Five thousand people who had come to listen to Jesus became hungry.

Jesus wanted to feed them. He asked if anybody had any food. One boy said he had five loaves of bread and two fish. Jesus asked the boy to bring them to Him. The boy did.

Jesus blessed and multiplied the loaves so that He was able to feed 5,000 people. There were even twelve baskets of leftovers!

This is a joyful service that is used when we are remembering a happy event such as the feast day of a favorite saint.

Jesus did the miracle not only to show us His great power, but also to show us that He is the Bread of Life that feeds and satisfies far more than 5,000 people.

Jesus gives Himself to us as the Bread of Life every time we receive His Body and Blood in the Sacrament of Holy Communion.

I am the Bread of Life: he who comes to me shall not hunger, and he who believes in me shall never thirst (John 6:35).

The blessing of the five loaves reminds us of the miracle of the feeding of the five thousand.

The Table of Preparation

The **table of preparation** is a small table to the left of the altar.

It is behind the icon screen. This is the table on which the priest prepares the bread and wine for the liturgy.

During this service the priest pours wine and water into the chalice. He also removes from the loaf of bread the *Lamb of God* and other pieces of bread that stand for the Mother of God, the apostles, the saints, the living and the dead.

He places all these on the *paten*. (See the section on the PATEN in this book. It describes this beautiful service). The priest then covers the chalice and the paten with veils.

The veils stand for the swaddling clothes with which the baby Jesus was wrapped.

During the Great Entrance of the liturgy, the priest carries the chalice and the paten, covered with veils, from the table of preparation to the main altar table for the liturgy. This takes place in a special procession called The Great Entrance.

An icon of the Birth of Jesus is found near the table of preparation. This is because the table of preparation stands for the manger in Bethlehem where Jesus was born.

When we receive His Body and Blood in Holy Communion, Jesus comes to be born in the manger of our hearts. He becomes *Emmanuel: God with us.*

> **When Christ lives in us, we can say with St. Paul, "It is no longer I who live, but Christ who lives in me" (Gal. 2:20).**

The table of preparation reminds us of the
manger in Bethlehem where Jesus was born.

The Easter Candle

If you are visiting the church at Eastertime you will see a special candle called the **Paschal (Easter) candle**. This is kept on the holy altar table.

This candle stands for the risen Christ. It is lit in the darkened church for the Easter liturgy. It is held by the priest.

The people in church also hold candles. The priest invites the people to come and light their candles from the Paschal candle. He says to them, "Come receive light from the light that never dims, and give praise to Christ Who is risen from the dead."

When the liturgy is over, the people carry the lighted Easter candle home.

They make the sign of the cross on the front door of their house with the candle. Then they bless each room of the house with the holy light.

In order to keep the holy light in the house all year long, the Paschal candle is then used to light the small votive light that burns before the family icon.

During the forty days of Easter, Orthodox families light their Easter candles at the supper table as they sing:

> *Christ is risen from the dead. By his death he has destroyed death. And to those in the tombs He has given life.*

I am the resurrection and the life. He who believes in me will live, even though he dies; and whoever lives and believes in me will never die (John 11:25).

The Easter Candle: Christ is risen!

The Chandelier

If we look up in an Orthodox church we will often see a **chandelier** hanging from the dome or ceiling.

A chandelier is a beautiful collection of lights placed in the midst of cut glass and crystal. Together they sparkle with great beauty.

They remind us of the glorious beauty of the heavens with the sun, the moon, the planets, and the countless stars.

The chandelier reminds us that the heavens speak to us. They tell us of the greatness of God.

If the stars came out only once every one thousand years, we would stay up all night to see them. We would never forget what we saw.

But they come out every night to remind us of God's presence. We should not take them for granted. They tell of God's greatness. They show forth His glory.

Someone once called the moon "God's night light."

Every time we see the chandelier, it reminds us of how great God is. He is the One who placed all those beautiful stars in the heavens.

He is the One who guides them. He is also the One who loves and guides us when we place our lives in His hands.

> *O Lord, how manifold are Thy works! In wisdom hast Thou made them all (Psalm 104:24).*

Chandeliers remind us of the majesty of God and the beauty of the heavens.

The Baptismal Candle

When we see candles in church we should remember a very special candle that was given to us when we were baptized. It is called the **Baptismal Candle.**

This candle meant that the person baptized had received Christ Who is the Light of the World. When the priest would give this candle to the newly baptized person, he would repeat the words of Jesus, "Let your light so shine before people that they may see your good works and give glory to your Father in heaven" (Matt. 5:16).

The baptismal candle is much like the lamps used in the story Jesus told of the ten young girls. They were waiting to meet Jesus the Bridegroom. When the newly baptized person was given the lighted candle, he was told to be like the five wise young girls. These girls had enough oil to keep their lamps burning. Because of this, they were able to welcome the Bridegroom when He came in the middle of the night.

The baptismal candle is a sign of our faithfulness to Christ until He comes again. Among the ancient Greeks the runner who won the race was not the person who crossed the line in the shortest time. Rather, it was the person who crossed the finish line in the shortest time **with the torch still burning.**

Our goal as Christians is that we cross the finish line into eternal life one day with the light of our baptismal faith still shining brightly.

In the early church when the priest gave the candle to the newly baptized, he would say, "Receive this candle and keep it burning so that when the Lord comes, you may be welcomed into the joy of God's kingdom."

Let us walk in the light of the Lord (Isa. 2:5).

**Our goal as Christians is to cross
the finish line into eternal life with
the light of our baptismal faith
still shining brightly.**

Vestments

The priest wears special clothes for the liturgy. These are called **vestments**. They are:

A long linen robe called the *sticharion* or *alb*. This is "the robe of salvation and joy." It stands for the white robe every Christian receives at baptism.

Over the shoulders the priest wears a long, beautiful double strip of cloth called the *stole* or *epitrachelion*. The stole stands for the grace of God that is poured out upon God's priests.

Around his waist, the priest wears the *zone* or *belt*. This stands for the strength which God gives His servants. As the priest puts on the *zone* he prays, "Blessed is God Who girds me with strength ..."

Around his wrists the priest wears the cuffs or *epimanikia*. These cover the sleeves of the *alb*. They make it easier for the priest to move his hands during the liturgy. The cuffs stand for the power of God which flows into the priest's hands to help him serve God.

Lastly the priest puts on the *phelonion* or *chasuble*. This covers the whole body in the back and goes below the waist in the front. As the priest puts on the phelonion he prays that he be covered with all the righteousness of God.

St. John Chrysostom tells us that the vestments are there to hide the person of the priest. When we see the priest at the altar, we are to see Christ through the vestments.

It is really Jesus Who is teaching and blessing us through the priest.

Your priests, O Lord, shall be clothed with righteousness.

**Your priests, O Lord, shall be clothed
with righteousness.**

The Baptismal Font

As you walk around the church you will come to a **baptismal font**. It looks like a large bowl that stands on a pedestal. It is in this font or bowl that babies are immersed three times when they are baptized.

The baptismal font is like a mother's womb. It is from here that we are born as Christians.

God said of each one of us when the priest lifted us out of the baptismal font, "This is my beloved son/daughter whom I love very much." At baptism God took us into His arms and blessed us.

When we were baptized our godparent made certain promises to God for us. He promised to say no to the devil and to obey Jesus as God. When we grow up, we must make those promises to Jesus for ourselves.

When we were baptized God assigned a very special guardian angel to watch over us. That angel is always with us. He never leaves us. This shows that God loves us with a very personal love.

A beautiful white robe was given to us when we were baptized. The white clothes that we wear at baptism stand for the new life of purity. God washed us clean from sin in the waters of baptism.

He made us whiter than snow. He wants us to keep the white robe clean by asking God to forgive us whenever we do wrong.

We were marked with the sign of the cross at baptism to show that we belong to Christ. The mark of the cross sets us apart as belonging to the Lord Jesus.

After baptism we have a right to say to the devil, "Take your hands off me. I don't belong to you. I belong to Christ. I am His child, not yours."

We were therefore buried with Him through baptism into death in order that just as Christ was raised from the dead ... we too may live a new life (Rom. 6:4).

**At baptism God gives us a guardian angel
to watch over us.**

The Paten

The plate that holds the bread which becomes the body of Christ is called the **paten**.

The priest cuts out a large piece of bread and places it on the paten. It is stamped with the Greek initials IC, XC, NIKA. These Greek words mean JESUS CHRIST CONQUERS. This is the piece of bread that will be changed into the body of Christ. It is called the *Lamb of God.*

The priest then removes another piece of bread. This stands for the *Virgin Mary.* He places it on the paten on the left side of the Lamb of God.

Then he cuts out nine smaller pieces from the loaf. He places them on the paten on the right of the *Lamb of God.* These stand for the angels, prophets, apostles, and saints.

Then the priest cuts out a small piece of bread for each living person for whom he is praying. He places these pieces just below the *Lamb of God.*

Lastly, he cuts out a piece of bread for each deceased person he is remembering in prayer. He places these pieces on the paten just below or beside those of the living.

When finished, the whole church is gathered around the *Lamb of God* (Jesus) on the paten. Both the living and the dead are there because to God even the dead are alive.

In each liturgy we can place ourselves and our loved ones on the paten to be with Jesus and all the saints.

We can do this by giving the priest a list of names—living and dead—for whom we request prayer.

> ***Pray for each other so that you may be healed. The prayer of a righteous man is powerful and effective (James 5:16).***

70

The whole Church is gathered on the paten around the Lamb of God.

The Diptych or Priest's Prayer List

On the altar of preparation where the bread and wine are prepared for the liturgy, the priest keeps what is called a **diptych**.

This is a list of names of the people—living as well as dead—for whom the priest prays before each liturgy.

As we read in the section on the *paten*, the priest removes a piece of bread from the *prosphora*, or offering bread, for each person for whom he prays.

He places this bread on the paten just below the *Lamb of God,* the Lord Jesus.

If we wish to place ourselves on the paten with Jesus, the *Lamb of God*, and all the apostles and saints, we can have our family prepare a *diptych*, a family prayer list for the priest.

It can be done as attractively as possible with the name of your family on the front cover.

On the inside there should be two columns of names. One for the dead and one for the living.

The priest will keep your family prayer list (*diptych*) on the table of preparation. This will remind him to pray for your family before each liturgy.

> *In nothing be anxious but in everything by prayer and supplication with thanksgiving, let your requests be made known to God. And the peace of God which passes all understanding will keep your minds and hearts in Christ Jesus (Phil 4:6-7).*

Include your loved ones on the priest's prayer list

The Bishop's Throne

The **bishop's throne** is located to the right of the icon screen. It is set apart for the bishop who is the leader of the church. The bishop represents Jesus Christ. For this reason an icon of Christ, the High Priest, is placed on the bishop's throne.

The bishop sits or stands at the throne during church services. He blesses the people. Often he speaks to the people from his throne. When we see the bishop at his throne, we feel that we are in the presence of Jesus.

The bishop holds a pastoral staff. This is like a shepherd's staff. It is a staff that has a loop at one end. The shepherd uses this staff to lead the straying sheep back into the sheepfold.

The bishop holds this staff to show that, like Jesus, he is the good shepherd who cares for the flock and leads them to the safety of the sheepfold which is the church.

When the bishop celebrates the liturgy, he blesses us with two candlesticks. One is a triple-branched candlestick which expresses our belief in the Trinity, that is, in the Father Who loves us, the Son Who saves us, and the Holy Spirit Who lives in us.

The double-branched candlestick expresses our belief that Jesus was both God and man in the same Person.

Holding the triple-branched candlestick in his right hand and the double-branched one in his left hand, the bishop prays God's blessing upon us.

God loves us. He shows us His love for us by blessing us through the bishop, the priest, our parents, and grandparents.

> *He tends his flock like a shepherd: He gathers the lambs in his arms and carries them close to his heart; He gently leads those that have young (Isa. 40:11).*

The bishop holds a pastoral staff to represent Jesus, the Good Shepherd.

The Bread Offering or Prosphora

Every Sunday there are people who bring a loaf of bread to church for the liturgy.

They bring the bread to show that Jesus is the bread of life. The Greek word for the gift of bread is **prosphora**. It means a gift or offering.

We bring bread also because it stands for life. It is the staff of life.

We cannot live without it. Once we eat bread, it becomes part of us—our flesh and bones.

So, when we bring bread to church for the liturgy, we are really giving our life to God. It is the gift of our love.

When the bread is placed on the altar, it becomes God's. God is so pleased with the gift of our life that He changes it through the Holy Spirit.

It becomes His precious Body. He gives it back to us.

And this is how Holy Communion takes place. We give ourselves to God through the bread and He gives Himself to us by changing our gifts of bread and wine into His precious Body and Blood.

We come to the liturgy not just to *receive* Christ, but also to *give* ourselves to Christ.

> *Present your bodies as living sacrifices, holy and pleasing to God. This is your spiritual act of worship (Rom. 12:1).*

Bringing bread to church is a gift of love. It represents the giving of our life to Christ.

Stained Glass Windows

In many Orthodox churches icons are placed in windows. These are called **stained glass windows**.

When the sun shines in through these windows, the icons on them come alive in all their beauty and color.

When a child was asked once, "What is a saint?" she answered, "A saint is someone who lets God's light shine through his life."

When we let the light of Jesus shine in our lives, we become like the saints on the stained glass windows.

Our lives become alive with the holiness and beauty of God.

We reflect the glory of God.

When people see this, they will want to come to Jesus to learn more about Him.

I will let the light and love of Jesus shine through my life.

Let the light of your face shine upon us, O Lord (Psalm 4:6).

When we let the light of Jesus shine in our lives, we glow like the saints in the stained glass windows.

The Blessing of Icons

Orthodox Christians pray in church. They pray also at home. This is why we have icons in church and icons at home.

The icon that we have at home becomes **a place of prayer when it is blessed by the priest in church.** It is not fully an icon until it is blessed. Then it carries with it the presence of God.

When we buy an icon for our home, we bring it to church first. We ask the priest to bless it.

After he blesses it, we take it home and place it on a special prayer table. This becomes the place for prayer in our home.

The prayer table may have also a Bible, or Bible story book, a prayer book, a vigil light or candle, a small home censer, a cross, a vase for flowers, and a small bottle of holy water.

The prayer table becomes a "little church" in our home.

Do you have a prayer table in your home? Where is it? Do you know the names of the saints on the icon(s)?

What other things do you keep on your prayer table? Do you pray there?

If you do not have a prayer table corner, ask your parents to help you make one.

Hear my prayer, O Lord; listen to my cry for mercy (Psalm 86:6).

**The prayer table becomes a "little church"
in our home.**

The Angels on the Altar

On either side of the tabernacle on the altar table are two round shields. They are called in Greek "exapteriga," meaning "six wings."

On these round shields one sees carvings of the **six-winged angels**. The prophet Isaiah saw these angels in a vision he had of heaven.

He wrote about it: "I saw the Lord sitting upon a throne, high and lifted up... Above Him stood the seraphim; each had six wings: with two he covered his face, and with two he covered his feet, and with two he flew. And one called to another and said, 'Holy, holy, holy is the Lord of Hosts; the whole earth is full of his glory'" (Isa. 6:1-3).

The round shields of the six-winged angels remind us that these same angels are present at the holy altar table which is God's throne on earth.

When we sing the hymn, "Holy, holy, holy... " during the liturgy the angels are singing it with us.

God wants us to be like the angels in praising Him and in serving as His messengers as we bring the message of God's love to the world.

Above Him stood the seraphim; each had six wings: with two he covered his face, and with two he covered his feet, and with two he flew (Isa. 6:1-3).

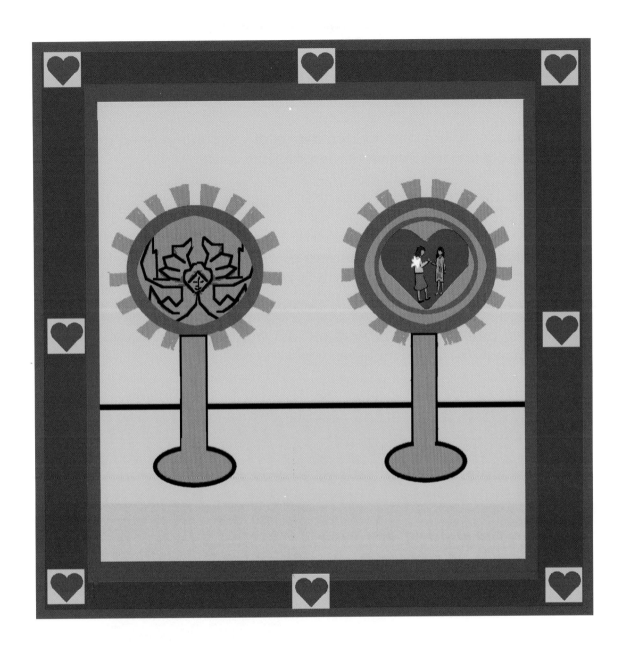

God wants us to be like the angels on the altar, praising Him and serving Him.

Two Large Candle Stands

Many Orthodox churches have **two large candle stands** before the icon screen.

These stands, full of candles, remind us of the column of light by which God guided the Jews to the promised land.

When the light appeared at night, God's people followed it until it led them to the promised land.

During the day God used a cloud to guide His people.

As the cloud of God's presence moved, they followed it.

These two candle stands remind us that we, too, have a promised land which is the kingdom of heaven.

Just as God guided His people, the Jews, to their promised land, so today He guides us to our promised land through Jesus who is our great Light.

When we follow Jesus, He leads us to heaven.

I am the light of the world. Whoever follows me will not walk in darkness, but will have the light of life (John 8:12).

When we follow Jesus, He leads us to heaven.

Sacrament of Confession

Just below the icon of Christ on the icon screen there is often a kneeler. This is where people meet the priest for the sacrament of forgiveness, which is called **confession.**

This is where we can come to tell Jesus about how sorry we feel for our sins. This is where we receive Christ's forgiveness.

When we kneel before the icon, we face Jesus, not the priest.

We do this to show that we are telling our sins to Jesus, not the priest. Jesus is the One who forgives us. The priest stands behind us as a witness for Jesus.

We tell Jesus the sins for which we are very sorry. The priest explains how we can overcome our sins with God's help.

We promise to do better. And with God's help, we will do better.

The priest then places his stole over us as he pronounces God's forgiveness upon us.

Then we hear those beautiful words, "(Your name), your sins are forgiven in the name of the Father and the Son and the Holy Spirit."

Jesus takes away our sins.

We leave feeling renewed and cleansed. We leave with the great joy of God's salvation in our hearts.

As far as the east is from the west, so far does He remove our transgressions from us (Ps. 103:12).

In the Sacrament of Confession we tell Jesus we are sorry for our sins and He forgives us.

The Chanter's Stand

Just outside the icon screen on the right hand side, there is usually a **chanter's stand**.

This is a stand on which the many prayer books of the church are kept. A group of readers and singers gathers around this stand to pray the prayers and sing the hymns for the worship services. The songs we sing in church are called hymns. The Greek word for hymn is Troparion.

Why do we sing in church?

We sing because God has filled us with joy. He has destroyed sin and death for us. When we ask for forgiveness, He forgives us. He lifts us up every time we fall. He invites us to call Him "Our Father."

He has opened the door to heaven for us.

Our joy is so great that we have to sing it out. Even the angels in heaven sing out their prayers of praise. Someone even said that when someone sings his prayers, he is praying twice.

Singing makes our prayers twice as strong.

Many times a choir helps the chanter sing. Many churches have a song book on each seat. This is called a hymnal.

Many worshippers are learning the hymns of the liturgy and are using the hymnal to sing the hymns along with the choir.

When we come to church to worship God, it is good that we all pray and sing together in praise of God.

Liturgy means the people of God working together, praying together, and singing together the praises of God.

Let us make a joyful noise unto the Lord, all the earth (Psalm 100:1).

Singing together the praises of God

Altar Servers

There is a special room in most Orthodox churches. It is a room full of closets, cupboards and drawers. All the important things that are used in the worship service are kept in this room.

It is the room where the **altar servers** keep the special robes they wear during the services. It is also the room where the priest keeps his vestments. This room is called the *sacristy*.

The altar server wears a robe called the *sticharion*. This is similar to the sticharion worn by the deacon and priest. It is the "robe of salvation" which we all receive at baptism.

When the server is elevated by the bishop to the office of reader, he receives an additional vestment called the *orarion*. This is like a stole which the reader wears around the sticharion. The orarion reminds us of the wings of the angels who pray around God's throne in heaven.

An altar server is one who prays with the priest in the altar. He helps the priest in many ways and takes part in the entrances and processions.

If you would like to be an altar server, ask your priest. He will be glad to tell you how you can help him as a server.

The altar servers wear special clothes for the liturgy. We, too, should come to worship God wearing the special clothes of forgiveness toward all, faith, love, and humble service to those in need.

St. Paul says, "As many as have been baptized in Christ have put on Christ." At baptism, God dressed us with the virtues of Jesus. The greatest of these is love. Let us wear the garment of love at all times.

Altar servers help the priest.

The Offering Baskets

As you walk around the church, you will see **offering baskets**.

These are passed from one person to another during the liturgy on Sundays. People place money in the baskets for God's work.

When we place money in the basket for God's work, it is like placing ourselves in the basket to be used by God.

The more we love God, the more we give to Him. Love gives, and gives, and gives again. In fact, true love never stops giving.

Many children bring a part of their allowance every Sunday and place it in the offering basket for God's work. They do this to show their love for God.

Some of this money is used to help the poor and the hungry, to help build new churches, to train new priests, to teach people about God and His love for us.

God gives us everything we have. He even gave His only Son for us on the cross.

Such love makes us want to give our lives and all that we have to Jesus.

God loves a cheerful giver (2 Cor. 9:7).

The more we love God, the more we give to Him.

Two Processions

One person tells of watching **two parades of people** on Sunday morning. One parade of people was going to church. A second parade of people was leaving church to go home.

They were the same people. They came to church sick, they left healed.

They came to church without hope, they left full of hope.

They came to church weak, they left strong.

They came to church as sinners, they left forgiven.

They came to church in darkness, they left in light.

They came to church hungry, they left filled.

They came to church sad, they left full of joy.

They had come to the living Christ and He had done a miracle for His people.

Next Sunday I, too, will be coming to church with my parents.

My presence in church will mean much more to me because of this brief walk I have taken through God's house.

Everything I see will be speaking to me about God. I thank God for this walk.

It has brought me closer to Jesus.

Come to me, all you who are weary and burdened, and I will give you rest (Matt. 11:28).

We come to church sad,
we leave full of God's joy.